WITHDRAWN

COOL SCIENCE

Experiments with Electricity and Magnetism

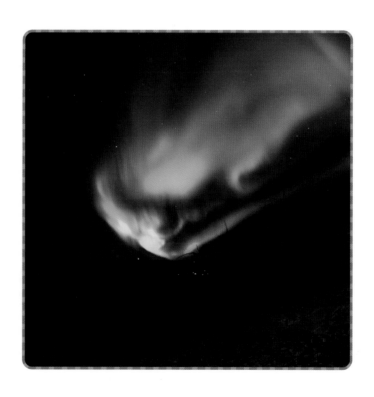

By Chris Woodford

Gareth Stevens
Publishing

Please visit our Web site www.garethstevens.com. For a free color catalog of all our high-quality books, call toll free 1-800-542-2595 or fax 1-877-542-2596.

Library of Congress Cataloging-in-Publication Data
Woodford, Chris.
    Experiments with electricity and magnetism / Chris Woodford.
        p. cm. -- (Cool science)
    Includes index.
    ISBN 978-1-4339-3444-5 (lib. bdg.) -- ISBN 978-1-4339-3445-2 (pbk.)
    ISBN 978-1-4339-3446-9 (6-pack)
    1. Electricity--Experiments--Juvenile literature. 2. Magnetism--Experiments--Juvenile literature.   I. Title.
QC533.W66 2010
537.078--dc22   2009037141

Published in 2010 by
Gareth Stevens Publishing
111 East 14th Street, Suite 349
New York, NY 10003

© 2010 The Brown Reference Group Ltd.

For Gareth Stevens Publishing:
Art Direction: Haley Harasymiw
Editorial Direction: Kerri O'Donnell

For The Brown Reference Group Ltd:
Editorial Director: Lindsey Lowe
Managing Editor: Tim Harris
Editor: Sarah Eason
Children's Publisher: Anne O'Daly
Design Manager: David Poole
Designer: Paul Myerscough
Production Director: Alastair Gourlay

Picture Credits:
Front Cover: Shutterstock: Roman Krochuk (background); Marilyn Volan (foreground)
Title Page: Shutterstock: Roman Krochuk
Shutterstock: Michael Chamberlain 6t, Oleksiy Fedorov 5, Martin Fisher 4, Martin Trajkovski 7, Yulli 6b
All other images Martin Norris

Publisher's note to educators and parents: Our editors have carefully reviewed the Web sites that appear on p. 31 to ensure that they are suitable for students. Many Web sites change frequently, however, and we cannot guarantee that a site's future contents will continue to meet our high standards of quality and educational value. Be advised that students should be closely supervised whenever they access the Internet.

Manufactured in the United States of America
1 2 3 4 5 6 7 8 9   12 11 10

CPSIA compliance information: Batch #BRW0102GS: For further information contact Gareth Stevens, New York, New York at 1-800-542-2595.

Contents

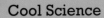

Introduction

It is hard to imagine a world without electricity and magnetism. There would be no computers, the motors that drive machines would stop, and all the lights would go out.

A bolt of lightning lights up the night sky. Lightning is caused by the buildup of electricity in storm clouds.

Electricity and magnetism are fundamental forces of nature. They have existed ever since the universe was created billions of years ago. They shape everything around us. Electricity is the force that holds atoms together. These building blocks of matter make up everything from planets and stars to the bodies of animals and plants. Magnetism is the invisible force that keeps a compass needle pointing toward the magnetic north and holds magnets on the refrigerator door.

Scientists have only been experimenting with electricity and magnetism for a few hundred years. In this book you can try out some experiments with electricity and magnetism for yourself. Doing experiments is a fun way to find out about science.

What is electricity?

Everything in the universe is made up of tiny particles called atoms. Even smaller particles, called protons and neutrons, are found in the center of atoms. Protons have a tiny positive charge. Neutrons are about the same size as protons but have no charge. Even smaller particles, called electrons, have a tiny negative charge. They spin around the protons and neutrons in an atom, just like planets spinning around the Sun in the Solar System.

In most atoms, there are equal numbers of electrons and protons. This balances the negative and positive charges, making the atom neutral. Sometimes the balance is upset and a substance becomes charged. When an object is charged, it tries to attract charged particles to become neutral again. Everything to do with electricity is caused by these charged particles. When you switch on a flashlight, for example, electricity flows from the battery to the bulb. The electricity makes the bulb heat up and glow, providing the light you need to see in the dark.

Different forms

There are two different forms of electricity: static electricity and current electricity. Static electricity is caused when charged particles build up in one place.

Electricity pylons and overhead cables carry electricity from the power station to your home so you can watch television and play computer games.

LEARNING ABOUT SCIENCE

Doing experiments is the best way to learn about science. This is the way scientists test their ideas and find out new information. Follow this good science guide to get the most out of each experiment in this book.

• Never begin an experiment until you have talked to an adult about what you are going to do.
• Take care when you do or set up an experiment, whether it is dangerous or not. Make sure you know the safety rules before you start work. Wear goggles and use the right safety equipment when you are told to do so.
• Do each experiment more than once. The more times you carry out an experiment, the more accurate your results will be.
• Keep a notebook to record the results of your experiments. Make your results easy to read and understand. You can make notes and draw charts, diagrams, and tables.
• Drawing a graph is a great way of presenting your results. Plot the results of your experiment as dots on a graph. Use a ruler to draw a straight line through all the dots. Reading the graph will help you to fill in the gaps in your experiment.
• Write down the results as you do each experiment. If one result seems different from the rest, you might have made a mistake that you can fix immediately.
• Learn from your mistakes. Some of the most exciting findings in science came from an unexpected result. If your results do not agree with your predictions, try to find out why.

You can make static electricity by rubbing a plastic ruler against a cloth. The cloth rubs off some of the electrons from the ruler. The electrons build up on the cloth, which becomes negatively charged. The plastic ruler loses electrons and becomes positively charged. The charges stay put until they come into contact with an object with an opposite charge. That is why this form of electricity is called static electricity—the charges do not move.

Current electricity is caused by the movement of charged particles. The movement of electrons through the flashlight is an example of current electricity. So is the electricity that powers everyday household devices such as computers and televisions.

Magnetism at work

Most people have seen a magnet at work. The most familiar magnet is the compass needle that helps people

A horseshoe magnet attracts other magnetic materials, such as these steel pellets.

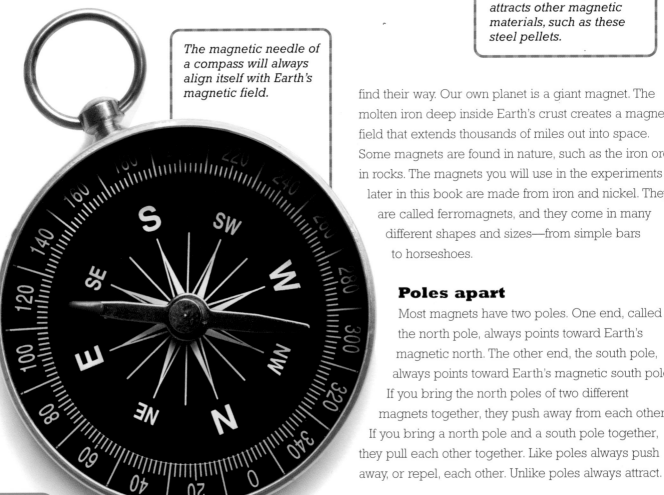

The magnetic needle of a compass will always align itself with Earth's magnetic field.

find their way. Our own planet is a giant magnet. The molten iron deep inside Earth's crust creates a magnetic field that extends thousands of miles out into space. Some magnets are found in nature, such as the iron ores in rocks. The magnets you will use in the experiments later in this book are made from iron and nickel. They are called ferromagnets, and they come in many different shapes and sizes—from simple bars to horseshoes.

Poles apart

Most magnets have two poles. One end, called the north pole, always points toward Earth's magnetic north. The other end, the south pole, always points toward Earth's magnetic south pole. If you bring the north poles of two different magnets together, they push away from each other. If you bring a north pole and a south pole together, they pull each other together. Like poles always push away, or repel, each other. Unlike poles always attract.

BE SAFE!

Electricity is powerful and dangerous. Many people lose their lives by not properly respecting the power of electricity. The experiments in this book are all safe if you follow the instructions very carefully in each one. If you are ever in any doubt about what to do, ask an adult to help you.

Magnetic field

The magnetic field is the area in which a magnet's effect operates. The magnetic field is strongest at the poles of the magnet and gets weaker farther away from the poles. Earth's magnetic field, or magnetosphere, extends around 40,000 miles (64,000km) into space on the side that faces the Sun. A stream of charged particles, called the solar wind, blows Earth's magnetic field far out into space. So, on the other side, the magnetosphere extends up to 160,000 miles (257,000km) into space.

Electromagnetism

Scientists used to think that electricity and magnetism were two different forces. Now they know that electricity and magnetism are actually part of the same force, called electromagnetism. Electricity always produces magnetism, and magnetism always produces electricity.

Scientists only found out about electromagnetism in the early nineteenth century. Danish scientist Hans Ørsted (1777–1851) discovered that switching on electrical equipment in his laboratory made a compass needle move. When he switched the equipment off again, the needle swung back to its original position. Ørsted realized that the electricity flowing through the electrical equipment created a magnetic field that deflected the compass needle.

Many scientists started doing experiments with electricity and magnetism when they heard about Ørsted's discovery. Soon they found that they could make powerful electromagnets by coiling a wire around an iron bar and attaching the wire to a battery.

Scientists do not fully understand why electricity and magnetism are so closely linked, but they have found many important uses. Powerful electromagnets can be used to lift heavy loads, such as scrap metals in a junkyard. And just as electricity produces a magnetic field, magnetism can be used to create electricity. This is called electromagnetic induction. It can be used to generate the electricity we need to light up our homes and provide power for electrical machines.

MAGNETIC LEVITATION

One unusual use of electromagnetism is as a power source for high-speed trains. Magnetically levitated (maglev) trains can reach speeds of more than 300 miles (480 kilometers) per hour. The train can move so fast because there are no wheels touching the track, so there is no friction to slow down the train. Instead, electromagnets inside the train make it "float" on a magnetic field above the guide rail.

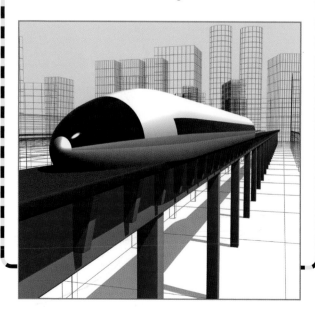

Lemon Battery

Goals

1 Use a lemon to build a battery.

2 Find out about electricity.

3 Measure how much electricity your lemon battery makes.

What you will need

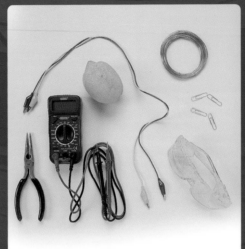

- fresh lemon
- copper wire
- paper clips
- wire clippers
- voltmeter or ammeter
- 2 electric leads with alligator clips at both ends
- safety goggles

LEVEL of Difficulty   ✪ Hard   ✪ Medium   ✪ Easy

2 Ask an adult to help you cut a 2-inch (5-cm) piece of copper wire using the wire clippers. Gently push the wire about 1 inch (2.5cm) into the lemon.

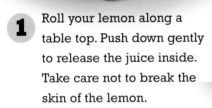

1 Roll your lemon along a table top. Push down gently to release the juice inside. Take care not to break the skin of the lemon.

3 Straighten out a paper clip. Gently push the paper clip about 1 inch (2.5cm) into the lemon. Position the paper clip as close to the copper wire as you can without actually touching it.

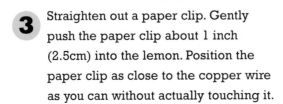

SAFETY TIP!

The lemon will not make enough electricity to hurt—but take care when touching the wires with your tongue so that you don't cut yourself.

AMMETERS AND VOLTMETERS

An ammeter measures electric current and displays it in amps. A voltmeter measures voltage and displays it in volts. There are two different types of ammeters and voltmeters. Some of them have pointers that swing across a dial. When a current passes through this type of meter, it creates magnetism. This makes the pointer move like a compass needle. Other meters have digital displays (like the one we have used in this activity). They measure current and voltage using electronic circuit boards instead of magnetism.

4 Roll your tongue around your mouth so it is wet. Gently touch both wire electrodes with your tongue at the same time. You should feel a slight tingling sensation. The lemon battery has made electricity, which is flowing through your tongue!

5 Use one of the electric leads with alligator clips to connect one end of the voltmeter or ammeter to the paper clip. Use another lead with alligator clips to connect the other end of the meter to the copper wire. If the meter shows a negative number, the circuit is the wrong way round. Swap the connections. Record the reading in your notebook.

TROUBLESHOOTING

What if I can't feel a tingling sensation in my tongue?

Make sure you are using a fresh, moist lemon. You may have to try different lemons before you get a nice juicy one that works. Place the wires very close together, and make sure your tongue is moist before touching the wires. Using a thicker copper wire will make it easier to feel the electricity.

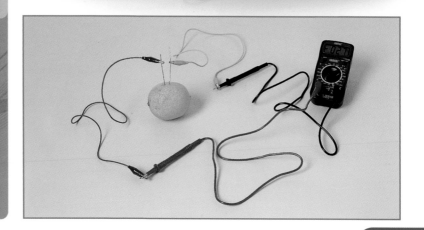

Voltaic Pile

What you will need

- paper towel
- scissors
- lemon juice
- 2 plastic plates
- 2 electric leads with alligator clips at both ends
- 5–10 pennies
- 5–10 dimes
- voltmeter

Goals

1 Make a simple battery called a voltaic pile.

2 Make electricity using pennies and dimes as electrodes and lemon juice as an electrolyte.

3 Measure the results using an ammeter or voltmeter.

LEVEL of Difficulty Hard Medium Easy

1 Cut the paper towel into squares, about 1 inch (2.5cm) across. You will need between five and ten pieces of paper towel.

2 Soak the paper squares in lemon juice.

SAFETY TIP!

Take care when using scissors. Always cut away from your body.

3 Clip one end of the electric wire to one of the pennies. Then build up a pile of coins and paper squares on top of it. Start with a penny, then a paper square, then a dime, then another paper square, and so on. If you start with a penny, the last coin in your coin pile should be a dime. To begin with, just use five pennies and five dimes.

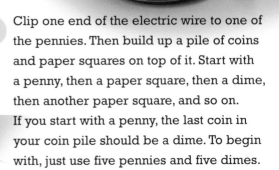

4 Clip another electric wire to the dime at the top of your pile.

TROUBLESHOOTING

What if my voltaic pile doesn't work?

The current may not have been flowing through some parts of the circuit. To fix this, first, try cleaning the coins. Then make sure all the parts of the pile are touching one another. Finally, check that all the pieces of paper towel are thoroughly soaked with the lemon juice.

5 Make sure all the layers of the pile are touching. You may need to press them together firmly. Connect the free ends of the wires to the ammeter or voltmeter. If the meter shows a negative number, the circuit is the wrong way round. Swap the connections. Record the result in your notebook.

MEASURING VOLTAGE AND CURRENT

Voltage is measured in units called volts (V), named for Italian scientist Alessandro Volta (1745–1827). A household battery produces a voltage of around 1.5 V, a car battery produces around 12 V, and the electricity supply that flows into most homes is 110 V.

Current is measured in units called amperes or amps (A), named for French scientist André-Marie Ampère (1775–1836). A current of 1A is quite large. The currents used in the experiments in this book are just a few milliamps (thousandths of an amp).

6 Repeat the experiment using more coins. In each case record the result. The reading gets larger the more coins you use. Why is this?

7 If you do not have an ammeter, just touch the ends of the alligator clips in a dark room. You should see a small spark. How does the spark change if you add more coins to the pile?

Electroscope

Goals

1 Build a device called an electroscope to create static electricity.

2 Use your electroscope to store the static electricity.

LEVEL of Difficulty ★ Hard ★ Medium ★ Easy

What you will need

- glass jar
- card
- pencil
- scissors
- thick metal wire 5–6 inches (13–15cm) long
- aluminum foil
- sticky tape
- plastic comb

1 Put the jar upside down on top of the cardboard. Draw a circle around the rim of the jar. Cut out the circle.

SAFETY TIP!

Take your time when bending the wire to avoid piercing your skin.

2 Bend the wire into a loop. Stick the ends of the wire through the card circle. Make sure the ends stick out by about 1 inch (2.5cm).

GOLD-LEAF ELECTROSCOPE

An electroscope is good at detecting static electricity. The best electroscopes use gold leaf instead of aluminum foil. Gold leaf is lighter than aluminum foil, and it conducts electricity better. This is why the gold-leaf electroscope can detect smaller amounts of static electricity.

3 Squash a piece of aluminum foil into a ball. Stick it on top of the wires.

4 Cut a strip of foil about 4 inches (10cm) long and ½ inch (1cm) wide. Bend the strip in half, and hang it over the wire loop. The two halves of the foil should not touch. Tape the lid onto the jar. The foil should hang in the center of the jar, without touching the glass.

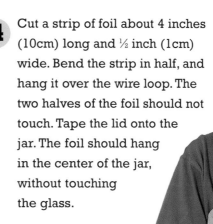

5 Rub the plastic comb five or ten times on your hair. Bring the comb near to the foil ball on top of your electroscope. The two ends of the foil will rise. The closer the comb, the more they rise.

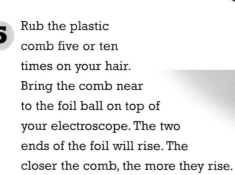

6 Hold the comb near the foil ball. Touch the foil ball with your other hand, and then take it away again. The two ends of the foil strip should fall back down. Then move the comb away from the electroscope. The foil strip will rise again and stay there. Can you think why this is?

TROUBLESHOOTING

What if the foil doesn't move?

Use the thinnest aluminum foil you can find. If foil from the kitchen does not work, try using the thin foil wrapping from a candy bar instead.

Leyden Jar

What you will need

- plastic container with a lid
- aluminum foil
- PVA glue
- metal screw
- metal door knob
- copper wire
- thin wire
- wire clippers
- 1-foot (30-cm) PVC pipe
- cotton cloth

Goals

1 Build a Leyden jar.

2 Store electricity in your Leyden jar.

3 Create a small bolt of lightning.

LEVEL of Difficulty

 Hard   Medium   Easy

2 Glue an identical strip of foil around the outside of the plastic container.

1 Tear a strip of aluminum foil big enough to wrap around the inside of the plastic container. Glue the foil to the inside of the container so it attaches smoothly to the plastic. Leave a gap of uncovered plastic at the top of the container.

3 Ask an adult to help you push the screw halfway through the plastic lid. The head of the screw should be on the inside of the container. The pointed end should stick out of the lid far enough to screw the metal knob onto it. Cut a 6-inch (15cm) length of copper wire. Wrap one end of the wire around the head of the screw. Tape the other end of the wire to the foil inside the container.

SAFETY TIP!

Some glue, such as rubber cement, is flammable. This means it catches fire easily. Do not use flammable glue in this experiment. Ask an adult to help you chose the right glue that is safe to use.

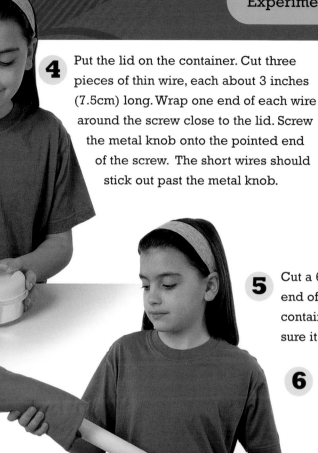

4 Put the lid on the container. Cut three pieces of thin wire, each about 3 inches (7.5cm) long. Wrap one end of each wire around the screw close to the lid. Screw the metal knob onto the pointed end of the screw. The short wires should stick out past the metal knob.

SAFETY TIP !

Although it is fun to make sparks, it can be dangerous. The bigger the spark, the higher the voltage. Large Leyden jars are big enough to store dangerous voltages, so use only a small container. Do not ever play with electricity.

5 Cut a 6-inch (15-cm) length of wire. Stick one end of the wire to the foil on the outside of the container. Leave the other end free, but make sure it touches the table.

6 Rub the PVC pipe with the cloth. Lightly touch the PVC pipe onto the short wires sticking out from under the knob on top of the jar. Repeat this step five times to charge your Leyden jar.

7 Put down the pipe. Pick up the free end of the wire taped to the outside foil. Bring it near the metal knob. Look closely. A tiny spark should fly across the gap between the wire and the knob.

TROUBLESHOOTING

What if I don't get a spark?

You may need to charge the jar more. Try repeating step 6 a few more times.

On a humid (moist) day the air conducts electricity away from the jar. This means that electric charge may leak out of your jar through the air as quickly as you put it in. Try to do the experiment on a dry day.

Electric charges leak away at sharp points. That is why it is important to cover the plastic container with very smooth foil. Also, make sure you stick the foil to the container as tightly as you can.

Fitting a Fuse

What you will need

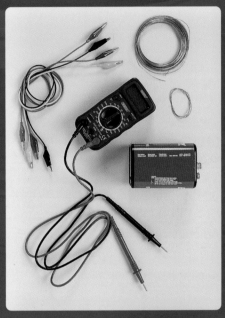

- thin iron wire, such as piano wire
- thin copper wire
- 3 electric leads with alligator clips at both ends
- 6V or 12V battery
- ammeter

Goals

1 Make your own fuse.

2 Compare different fuse materials in a circuit.

LEVEL of Difficulty   Hard   Medium   Easy

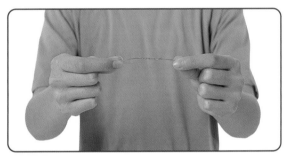

1 Cut a 2-inch (5-cm) length of copper wire and a 2-inch (5-cm) length of iron wire. Twist them together at one end to make a longer wire.

2 Take a lead, and attach one alligator clip to the free end of the iron wire. Attach the other end of the lead to one terminal of the battery.

3 Clip a second lead onto the free end of the copper wire.

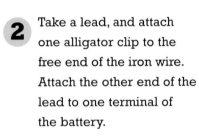

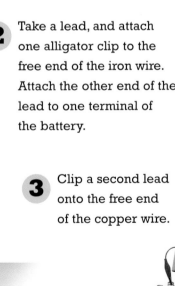

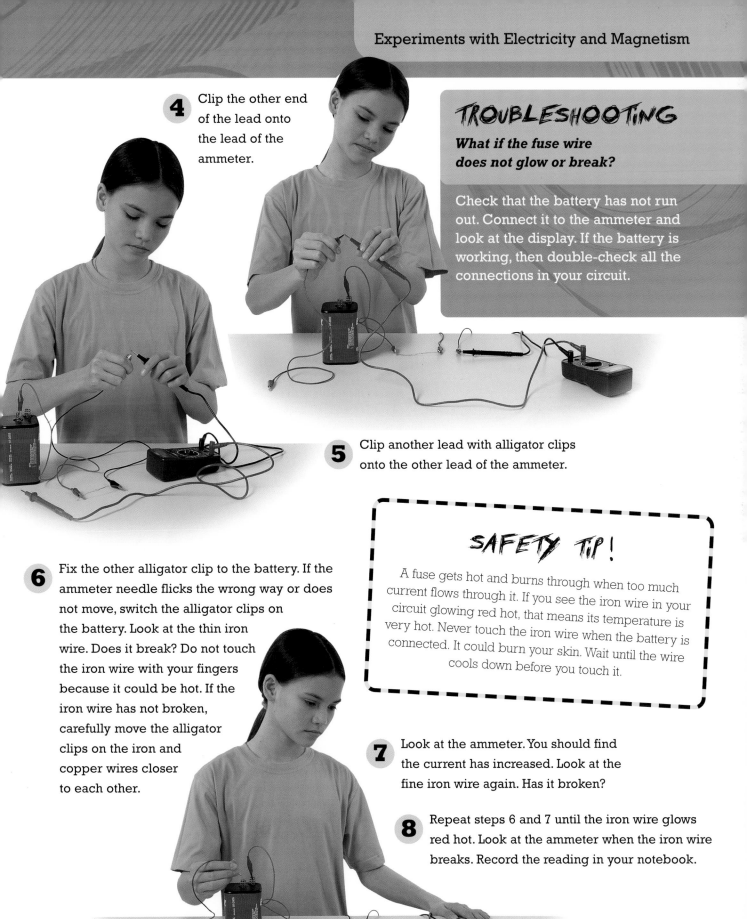

4 Clip the other end of the lead onto the lead of the ammeter.

TROUBLESHOOTING

What if the fuse wire does not glow or break?

Check that the battery has not run out. Connect it to the ammeter and look at the display. If the battery is working, then double-check all the connections in your circuit.

5 Clip another lead with alligator clips onto the other lead of the ammeter.

SAFETY TIP!

A fuse gets hot and burns through when too much current flows through it. If you see the iron wire in your circuit glowing red hot, that means its temperature is very hot. Never touch the iron wire when the battery is connected. It could burn your skin. Wait until the wire cools down before you touch it.

6 Fix the other alligator clip to the battery. If the ammeter needle flicks the wrong way or does not move, switch the alligator clips on the battery. Look at the thin iron wire. Does it break? Do not touch the iron wire with your fingers because it could be hot. If the iron wire has not broken, carefully move the alligator clips on the iron and copper wires closer to each other.

7 Look at the ammeter. You should find the current has increased. Look at the fine iron wire again. Has it broken?

8 Repeat steps 6 and 7 until the iron wire glows red hot. Look at the ammeter when the iron wire breaks. Record the reading in your notebook.

Curie Point

Goals

1 Heat a paper clip until it reaches its Curie point.

2 Use heat to make a material lose its magnetism.

LEVEL of Difficulty
☆ Hard ☆ Medium ☆ Easy

What you will need

- 2 tripods
- strong, round magnet
- string
- paper clip
- 6V battery
- 2 electric leads with alligator clips at both ends

SAFETY TIP!
The paper clip gets very hot in this experiment so do not touch it.

2 Use string to tie the paper clip between two legs of the other tripod. The paper clip should be level with the magnet hanging from the other tripod.

1 Use a piece of string to hang a magnet from one of the tripods.

3 Move the two tripods together until the magnet attracts the paper clip and sticks to it.

TROUBLESHOOTING

Why didn't the magnet fall away from the paper clip?

The battery you used might not have had enough voltage to heat the paper clip to its Curie point. You could use a stronger battery or try a thinner piece of iron or steel wire instead.

WHY iS EARTH MAGNETiC?

The molten iron inside Earth's core is extremely hot, but Earth is still magnetic. No one knows why. One theory is that electric currents circulate inside Earth's liquid core and create a magnetic field as they move.

4 Clip electric leads to each end of the paper clip. Clip the other ends of the leads to the terminals of the battery. It does not matter which way you connect them.

5 As the paper clip heats up, the magnet falls away from the paper clip. The clip is so hot that it has lost its magnetism. This temperature is called the Curie point.

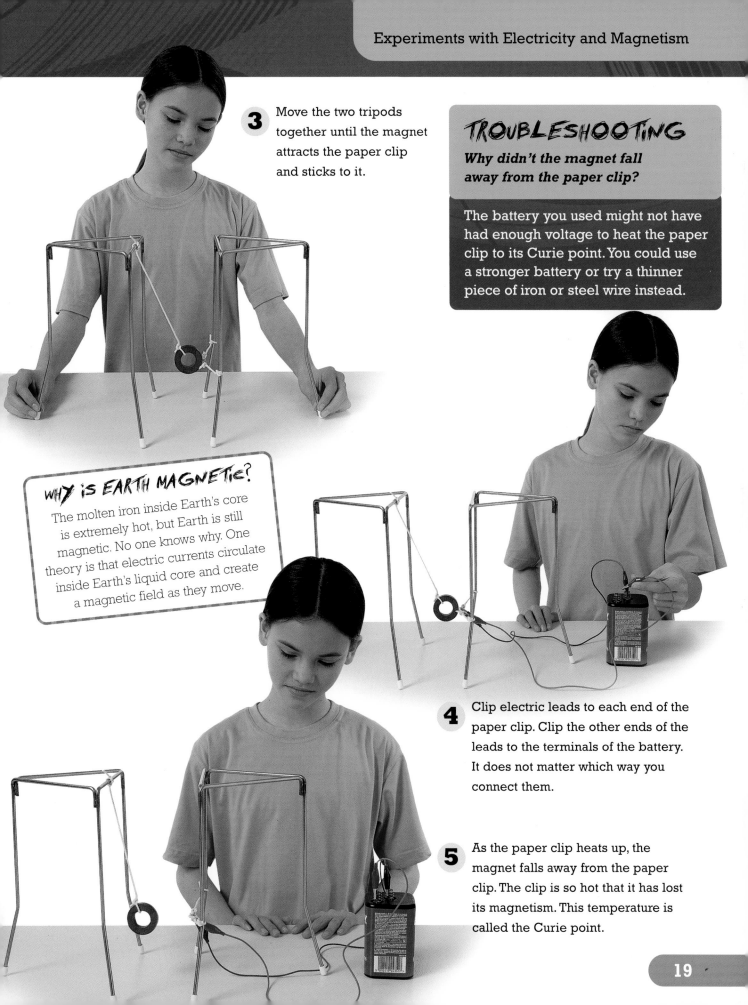

Motor Effect

Goals

1 Make a simple electric motor and use it to move a wire.

2 Use Fleming's left-hand rule to predict how your motor will move.

What you will need

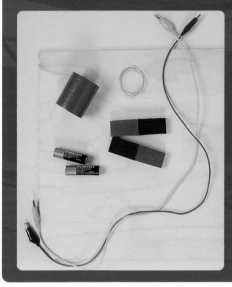

- wooden board
- strong tape
- 2 batteries (1.5V)
- 2 powerful bar magnets
- wire clippers
- thin iron wire, such as piano wire
- 2 electrical wires with alligator clips at both ends

LEVEL of Difficulty Hard Medium Easy

1 Tape the two batteries to the board so that the positive terminal of one battery touches the negative terminal of the other battery. The two 1.5V batteries are now the same as one 3V battery.

2 Tape the two bar magnets to the board. The north pole of one magnet should face the south pole of the other magnet. Leave a gap of about ½ inch (1cm) between them.

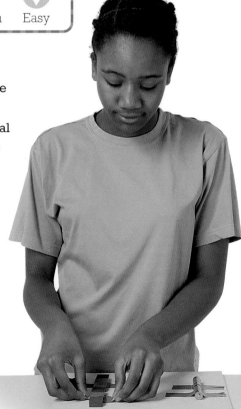

3 Cut a 2-inch (5-cm) length of wire. Clip one lead to each end of the wire. Place the wire in the middle of the gap between the two bar magnets.

TROUBLESHOOTING

How can I make the wire move by a larger amount?

Make sure you put the magnets the right way round. The poles that face each other need to be opposite— one north and one south. This means the field is very strong and at right angles to the wire. Setting up the magnets in this way will create the most powerful magnetic force to pull on the wire.

4 Clip the other ends of the leads to the battery terminals. Watch what happens to the wire. It should move a little.

5 Swap the connections on the batteries. Which way does the wire move now?

FLEMING'S LEFT-HAND RULE

Use Fleming's left-hand rule to predict which way the wire will move. Hold your left hand with the thumb, first, and second fingers at right angles. Point your first finger in the direction of the magnetic field (from north to south). Point your second finger in the direction of the current flow. Your thumb points in the direction of wire movement.

direction of wire movement

direction of magnetic field

direction of current

Changing Magnetic Field

What you will need

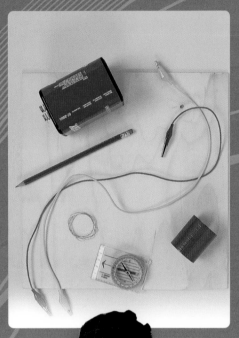

- thick card
- 4-inch (10-cm) length of wire
- 2 electric leads with alligator clips at both ends
- 6V battery
- compass
- pencil
- different colored pens
- strong tape

Goals

1 Create a magnetic field.

2 Use a compass to find the lines of magnetic force.

LEVEL of Difficulty

 Hard

 Medium

 Easy

SAFETY TiP!

Take care not to pierce your skin when you bend the metal wire.

1 Bend the wire into a "V" shape.

2 Tape the wire to the board with the ends of the "V" sticking up.

3 Clip one lead to each end of the wire.

4 Clip the other end of each lead to the terminal of a battery.

DISCOVERING ELECTROMAGNETISM

Danish physicist Hans Christian Ørsted (1777–1851) did this experiment in 1820. It showed that magnetism can be produced using electricity. It led to the idea that electricity and magnetism are two parts of the same thing, called electromagnetism. Later, English scientists Michael Faraday (1791–1867) and James Clerk Maxwell (1831–1879) developed the laws of electromagnetism.

5 Put your compass on the card. Move it slowly toward the wire. As you move the compass around, use a pencil to draw arrows on the board at different points. The arrows mark the direction of the compass needle.

6 Swap the connections. Put the compass at the same points as before. Use a colored pen to draw an arrow at each point. This shows the direction of the compass needle again. Make a note of how the direction has changed.

TROUBLESHOOTING

Why couldn't I find a magnetic field around the wire?

The magnetic field around the wire could be weak. It might not attract the compass needle. Increase the strength of your magnetic field by using more batteries. Make sure there are no other sources of electricity or magnetism nearby.

Build an Electromagnet

Goals

1 Build an electromagnet and test its strength.

2 Demonstrate the laws of electromagnetism.

LEVEL of Difficulty

 Hard   Medium   Easy

What you will need

- iron nail
- copper wire, 12 inches (30cm) long
- 2 electric leads with alligator clips at both ends
- 10–30 paper clips

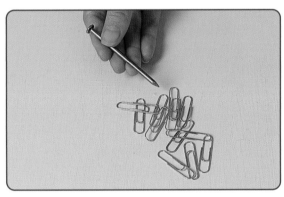

1 Hold up a nail to a pile of paper clips. You will not be able to pick up any paper clips with the nail because the nail is not magnetic.

2 Take a 12-inch (30-cm) length of copper wire. Coil it 20 times around an iron nail. Leave 2 inches (5cm) of wire sticking out at each end.

3 Clip an electric lead to each end of the wire. Connect each lead to the terminal of the battery.

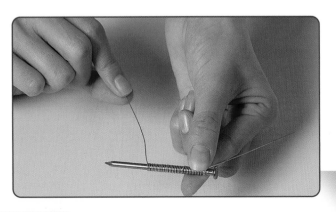

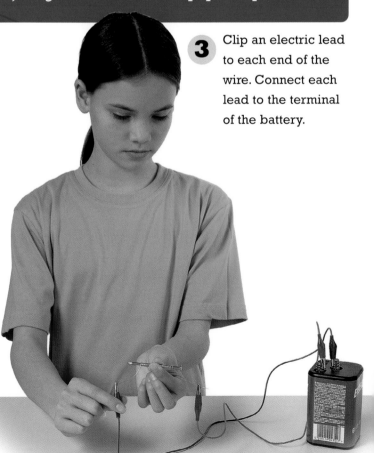

TROUBLESHOOTING

What if the nail electromagnet only picks up a few paper clips?

The electromagnet will be weak if there are not enough coils around the wire or if the coils are too loose. Start with another nail. Wrap at least 30 or 40 coils around the nail. Make sure you wind them very tightly.

4 Hold the nail close to the paper clips. Now it will pick up the paper clips. The nail has become an electromagnet.

5 See how many paper clips you can pick up.

ELECTROMAGNETIC GAUGES

A car fuel gauge uses an electromagnet to let the driver know how much gas is left in the tank. The electromagnet sits inside a permanent magnet in the fuel gauge. As current flows through the electromagnet, it turns toward the permanent magnet. This moves a pointer on the fuel gauge. The amount it turns depends on the strength of the current. A float inside the gas tank controls the current. It moves up and down with the level of gas. More current flows when there is more fuel in the tank. This creates a powerful electromagnet that pulls the pointer all the way over to read "FULL."

Eddy Currents

What you will need

- wooden dowel
- tripod
- string
- large bar magnet
- modeling clay
- disks made from different materials, such as badges, coins, buttons, and plastic lids
- stopwatch

Goals

1 Create eddy currents.

2 Compare the strength of the eddy currents created in different materials.

3 Use eddy currents to slow the movement of these materials.

LEVEL of Difficulty Hard Medium Easy

EDDY HEATING

Induction heating is a quick source of heat that can be used to process metals and other conductors. Current is sent through a coil. This generates a magnetic field. The metal to be processed is then put into the middle of the coil. The magnetic field creates eddy currents in the metal, heating it up. By varying the current, the metal can be heated to exactly the right temperature without touching the coil.

1 Ask an adult to drill a hole in one end of the dowel.

2 Thread string through the hole. Hang the dowel from the tripod so that it swings freely, like a pendulum. There should be about an inch between the end of the dowel and the table top.

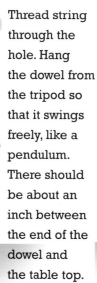

3 Put the magnet under the dowel. The dowel should hang over the middle of the magnet.

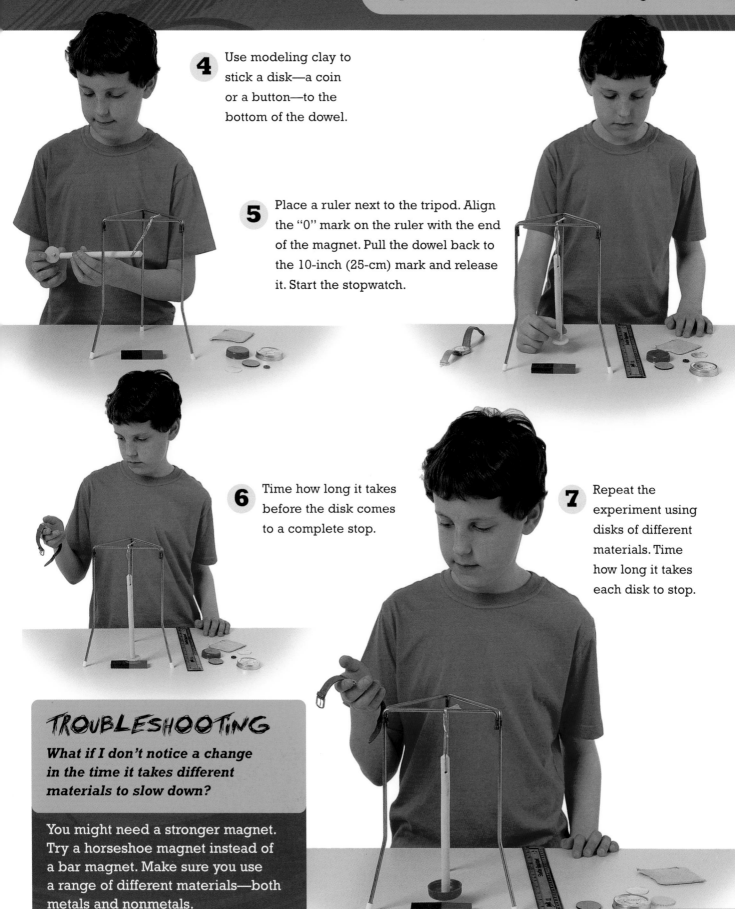

4 Use modeling clay to stick a disk—a coin or a button—to the bottom of the dowel.

5 Place a ruler next to the tripod. Align the "0" mark on the ruler with the end of the magnet. Pull the dowel back to the 10-inch (25-cm) mark and release it. Start the stopwatch.

6 Time how long it takes before the disk comes to a complete stop.

7 Repeat the experiment using disks of different materials. Time how long it takes each disk to stop.

TROUBLESHOOTING

What if I don't notice a change in the time it takes different materials to slow down?

You might need a stronger magnet. Try a horseshoe magnet instead of a bar magnet. Make sure you use a range of different materials—both metals and nonmetals.

Electroplating Metals

Goals

1 Use electricity to plate a thin layer of zinc onto copper.

LEVEL of Difficulty Hard Medium Easy

What you will need

- 2 pennies
- sandpaper
- pint of vinegar
- glass beaker
- toothbrush
- toothpaste
- a scale
- Epsom salts
- sugar
- 2 electrical leads with alligator clips at both ends
- 9V battery

1 Use sandpaper to sand down one of the pennies. Rub the surface of the penny until the dull gray zinc is exposed. It is easiest to sand the side of the coin.

2 Clean another penny with a toothbrush and some toothpaste until it is shiny. After cleaning, rinse the penny under the faucet.

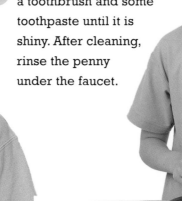

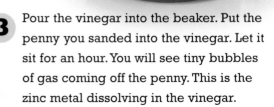

3 Pour the vinegar into the beaker. Put the penny you sanded into the vinegar. Let it sit for an hour. You will see tiny bubbles of gas coming off the penny. This is the zinc metal dissolving in the vinegar.

4 Remove the penny from the vinegar. Add 1½ ounces (43g) of Epsom salts and 2 ounces (57g) of sugar to the vinegar. Stir until it has dissolved.

5 Clip one lead to the cleaned penny and the second lead to the sanded penny.

TROUBLESHOOTING

Why doesn't my penny have a silvery coating?

Make sure the gray-colored zinc is showing through the penny you sand down. The penny should also bubble in the vinegar. There must be enough sugar and Epsom salts in the vinegar. Weigh them with scales to make sure. Check your battery. If it is flat, use a new battery. Try the activity again.

6 Put both pennies in the vinegar. Make sure they do not touch.

7 Connect the lead clipped to the clean penny to the negative terminal of the battery. Connect the other wire to the positive terminal. Disconnect the battery after 10 minutes. Carefully remove the pennies. The clean penny should have a silvery coating on it.

WATER ON THE MOON

Scientists are trying hard to find evidence of ice under the surface of the Moon, which could make building a base there much easier. The ice could be broken down, using electrolysis, into oxygen and hydrogen. People need oxygen to breathe, and hydrogen is a good fuel for making electricity. The two gases are also used as rocket fuel. Maybe one day a Moon base will be the first stop on expeditions to deep space.

Glossary

ammeter: a device used to measure current in units called amps

amp: the unit used to measure current

atoms: the tiny building blocks of all objects. Atoms are made up of protons, electrons, and neutrons.

charge: the particular amount of electricity in something

circuit: the path that electricity travels. Electricity can only flow around a complete circuit.

circuit board: a plastic board on which an electric circuit is laid out

conduct: to allow electricity to travel easily

current: the amount of a flow of electrical energy, or charge, in a substance. Currents are measured in amps.

electricity: the flow of electric power or charge. Electricity powers many of our machines, such as televisions, radios, and computers.

electrolysis: the use of an electrical current to bring about a chemical reaction

electromagnet: a core of magnetic material, such as iron, surrounded by a coil of wire. When an electric current is passed through the wire, the core becomes magnetic.

electron: a negatively charged part of an atom. Electricity is the flow of electrons.

ferromagnet: materials that are much more magnetic than most others

fuse: a wire, or thin metal, in an electric circuit that melts when too much electricity is flowing through it

levitate: to float above the ground

magnet: an object that can attract and hold magnetic materials

magnetic field: the area around a magnet where magnetism can be found

magnetic force: force exerted by something because of its magnetic energy

magnetism: the force that attracts or repels magnetic objects

motor: a machine that changes electrical or chemical energy into energy that can be used by a machine

molten: when a solid object has melted because of extreme heat

neutron: part of an atom

particle: a very tiny object

pole: one of the two ends of a magnet, the north and south poles

proton: a positively charged part of an atom

static electricity: an electric charge that does not move from one place to another

terminal: in batteries the places where electricity flows to and from

voltage: a measurement of potential difference

Further Information

BOOKS

Bailey, Jacqui. *Charging About: The Story of Electricity.*
London: A&C Black Publishers, 2004.

Trumbauer, Lisa. *What Is Electricity?* New York: Children's
Press, 2004.

Walker, Sally M. *Electricity.* Minneapolis, MN: Learner
Publications, 2006.

WEBSITES

www.eia.doe.gov/kids/energyfacts/sources/electricity.html

www.howstuffworks.com/electromagnete.htm

Index